IMMOVABLE

REFLECTIONS TO BUILD YOUR LIFE AND LEADERSHIP ON SOLID GROUND

MEREDITH KING

Immovable

Interior design:
www.doodles.blue

Published by:
NyreePress Literary Group
Fort Worth, TX 76161
1-800-972-3864
www.nyreepress.com

ISBN print: 978-1-945304-52-1

Library of Congress Control Number: pending
Categories: Non-Fiction / Memoir / Self-Help / Christian
Printed in the United States of America

To the amazing men and women who comprise the True to Life Ministries Team.

You consistently pour out your lives so people can find hope. Your dedication to excellence and commitment to create such a special sense of family inspires me every day. We are part of something special because we are part of God's story - today and forever more.

Forward

There are a number of experts readily available to tell you what to do and how to lead, and sometimes we need someone to just tell us what to do. I appreciate nitty-gritty how-to advice as much as the next gal, but that's not what this book is. I'm not coming to you as an expert, I'm coming as a friend, as someone in the trenches right alongside you.

The following pages reflect a life-long journey of messes. This is not a list of twenty things I've mastered - these are the topics you'll find on repeat in the tear-stained pages of my journals. I'm still learning and re-learning these truths, clinging to them for dear life. When life and leadership remind me I don't know what I'm doing, it's my cue to grow, to dig in, and most of all, to hit my knees.

As I think back on this wild journey so far, some of my most treasured moments have been at coffee shop tables or on living room couches with friends who really understand - who've walked this same beautiful and brutal road. Their nodding and understanding were pure refreshment to my soul. I hope you feel I'm with you as you read, just a friend sitting across the table, nodding and understanding.

Whether you are leading your family or a company, a ministry or a team, a few people or the masses, you belong here. I've prayed so much for you. That you would feel the Holy Spirit stirring your heart as you read, pray, and reflect. That His voice would speak to you, and that you'd find a fresh and steady confidence that comes from belonging to Christ. That you will find exactly what you need for the next step in your leadership journey, not in these pages, but in Him.

Honored to share this journey with you,

Meredith

How to Use This Book

Immovable: Reflections to build your life and leadership on solid ground includes twenty stand-alone chapters, unpacking foundational perspectives for leading well. They were designed to be daily readings, and are perfect for individual study or small group discussion.

1. Main Readings.
Short topical readings that set up the main topic and unpack a few central ideas.

2. Scripture.
Suggested reading to connect the theme directly to scripture.

3. Reflection.
Simple questions to capture your ideas and thoughts.

4. Today's Prayer.
Use these lines as a starting place to pray through the key ideas and applications of the day's topic. Incorporating scripture into prayer is a valuable, life-changing practice, and each day's scriptures were selected with this in mind. If this idea is new for you, please visit the online resource for Praying Scripture.

5. Practice.
Thoughtful exercises and applications to propel you into action.

Resources & Tips

Free Bonus Online Resources

In addition to all this little book contains, please register to receive access to free bonus chapters and other resources at:

www.immovablebook.com

Share Online

I believe your stories and experiences can help others grow and learn. I think God intended for us to share our journeys, even though we may be hundreds of miles apart. So, as you read and engage in the reflection and practice exercises, share your experiences with us on your social media platforms. And of course, I would love to connect with you. (You can most easily find me on Facebook and Instagram!)

Use the Hashtag:
#IMMOVABLEBOOK

Therefore, my beloved brothers,
be steadfast, immovable, always
abounding in the work of the
Lord, knowing that in the Lord
your labor is not in vain.

1 Corinthians 15:58 (HCSB)

Chapter List

Introduction

Let's start with the basic reality of leadership. Leading is incredibly hard and completely awesome, and no one has fully mastered it. Why? Because just about the time you think you've figured it out, the table turns. Seasons change. People come, and people go. You succeed, and then you fail. You win big and lose bigger. Opportunities knock and tragedies strike. Sometimes we respond with grace and dignity, and sometimes we turn into a big mess.

To complicate matters more, the world's messages are loud and compelling:

Do more.
Be more.
Fight for the top.
Figure it out.
Work harder.

We see the world holding up its own version of greatness, shining with notoriety, hustle, and outcomes, and it pulls on us because we were indeed made for greatness. But, the world's way is empty and exhausting, a poor imitation of the true greatness we were created for. There's nothing substantial there. Nothing to hold on to. And if we build our lives on a foundation of our own merits, accomplishments, and worthiness, when the storms of life come (and they always come), we will crumble. Fortunately, there's a better, higher way.

Have you ever driven through the mountains? I'm not talking about the tall hills so many fellow Texans point to and call "mountains." I'm talking about twisting and turning around enormous, rugged rocks abruptly bursting through the level earth in all sorts of majesty and glory, where around every bend is another breathtaking view of terrifying drop-offs, rushing streams, and lush valleys. I fell in love with the mountains of British Columbia as a young child, but what I feel toward them is far more than fascination. My heart yearns for those mountains and my soul craves them. The crystal blue sky, giant fir trees, and miles of beauty are unlike anything I've seen anywhere else.

Some of our dear friends live on the side of a mountain just outside my favorite postcard-worthy town. From their back porch, I can see mountains that start at the banks of a glistening lake and soar to over ten thousand feet in some places. My favorite sites aren't easy to get to. In fact, the travel is exhausting, but I keep going back whether I'm thirsty for adventure or desperate for rest.

My last trip marked the close of one of the most difficult seasons of my adult life. Grief, criticism, and betrayal knocked the wind out of me. Everything was changing, nothing was familiar or certain, and I felt like I was losing my way. I needed to feel solid ground under my feet. I needed to catch my breath. So, my husband did what any great husband would do; he bought us plane tickets and told me to pack my bags.

It wasn't enough for me to just look at the mountains from the valley, there was an urgency to get to the top, where I could sit in the silence of nature and look out over the earth. I knew from there all the buildings and houses and people that felt so big from the bottom would appear tiny. My whole perspective changed looking out from eight thousand feet. Surrounded by the enormity and strength of those majestic peaks, I felt appropriately small. I think one of the reasons I love the mountains so much is, they stand as bold beacons of God's character:

Steadfast.
Immovable.
Certain.
Resolute.

I returned home to find life very much the same. I knew I would. There was still plenty of chaos and trouble, but my heart was in a different place because I remembered that my world falling apart didn't mean I had to. I felt God holding me; His strength running through me. I knew even though everything was moving around me, He was holding on to me, and I was holding on to Him.

Our distracted, shaky, fight-for-the-top generation is

frantically trying to find what's lasting and real. It's as if we live in a perpetual identity crisis, trying out every possible answer to, "Who am I?" and "What's my purpose?" When one answer proves insufficient, we trade it in for another and another and another. When our eyes are fixed on our outward lives, success and value are measured by circumstances, but God is far more interested in the posture of our hearts. "The Lord does not look at the things people look at. People look at the outward appearance, but the Lord looks at the heart" (1 Samuel 16:7 NIV).

Leading well isn't determined by title, credentials, office size, relationship status, or your number of social media followers. It's not about perfection or achievement or applause. Whether you are leading from a boardroom or a playroom, whether your morning routine calls for a business suit or ball cap, God has positioned you to influence others and to lead people to Christ. He has given you gifts and talents to use for His glory and for His purposes. Maybe this is why leading feels like such a weighty responsibility. It feels bigger than we are, because it is.

The world may be in an identity crisis, but we are not. Our identity is settled. Our purpose is not a mystery. Because of Jesus and what He's done to rescue us, redeem us, and make us new, we are free from striving, free from chasing, free from our identities being tossed and shoved by circumstances and life. Friends, we aren't just living our story, we are part of God's story, and to fully lean into something greater, something eternal, our hearts and attention cannot be divided.

Our desire for greatness, for more than status quo,

isn't an accident or a mere product of our fast-paced society. God placed a deep-seated desire for greatness in our hearts, but it is only truly fulfilled by making Him great. Jesus tells us, "But the seed falling on good soil refers to someone who hears the word and understands it. This is the one who produces a crop, yielding a hundred, sixty or thirty times what was sown" (Matthew 13:23 NIV). We are made to produce fruit, to have an impact that multiplies, not just here and now, but for eternity.

God's stirring of that desire can help you plant a church, start a nonprofit, or launch a business. Or prompt you to sell all your possessions and move across the world. It may move you to invite friends and strangers to your table or to foster a child. But when the nonprofit seed money runs out, when plans completely fall apart, or when you feel exhausted from sleepless nights, you're going to need roots that go down deep. When your greatest fan becomes your loudest critic, when the rejection letter comes, or when the overwhelming need far outweighs the resources, your feet need solid ground. When everything shifts and moves, when life props you up and then let's you fall, you better be tied to something that's firmly established and unchanging.

So here we are. At the beginning. Starting this journey together. I wish I was on the other side, telling you how to lead and serve and follow Jesus from an expert's perspective. However, I know what I'm after.

It's found at the end of 1 Corinthians 15.

Therefore, my beloved brothers, be steadfast, immovable, always abounding in the work of the Lord, knowing that in the Lord your labor is not in vain.
(1 Cor. 15:58 ESV)

Such powerful words: Steadfast. Immovable. Abounding.

When your well-planned life or career doesn't work out, when criticism goes public, or when betrayal hits really close to home, I want you to know who you really are. When grief moves in like an unwanted roommate or finances are stretched thin, I want you to remember who you belong to. When the world applauds and props you up, I want you to be certain your identity isn't found there. Quiet confidence comes when you understand this world is not our home. So, I want your eyes and your life to be completely fixed on Jesus, firm in purpose, and unswayed by feelings and opinions.

I want your life to overflow with the work of the Lord, because it's all that lasts.

I want you to fully lean into your part in God's story of reconciliation and redemption, because our world is absolutely desperate for it.

I want your life and your faith and your purpose to be immovable.

I want all of that for me too.

We really like to measure things, but we are part of building an eternal glory that cannot be measured. It doesn't always make sense, and it may make us uncomfortable. (Okay, it WILL make us uncomfortable.) But, we were meant for this.

Identity

"You find peace not by rearranging
the circumstances of your life, but
by realizing who you are at the
deepest level."
- *Thomas Merton*

Our culture is in a perpetual identity crisis. Every time we've got identity, purpose, and belonging in our sights, trends change, opportunities end, people leave, or something unexpectedly falls apart, and we are left struggling to catch up. Are we our titles, our achievements, or our relationship status? Are we named by opinions, labels, or failures? What are we holding out in front of us as our trophy of worth? And how many trophies have been exchanged for bigger and better ones?

For about as long as I can remember, there's been a voice in my head saying, *"I'm not enough."* Picked last for kickball in kindergarten: *I'm not enough.* Not invited to the birthday party: *I'm not enough.* Overlooked for homecoming and prom dates: *I'm not enough.* I didn't know how to turn the volume down, so I tried to drown it out with achievement and hard work. I made perfect grades, grabbed every leadership position and internship I could, and planned a seamless transition into college as everyone cheered me on toward certain success. Two months into my freshman year, I got incredibly sick. While doctors spent months figuring out what was wrong, I spent months in bed, accumulating C's, D's, and F's in my classes. Christmas break was a nightmare. All my friends bragged about Dean's List recognition while I avoided eye contact, finding every imaginable reason to excuse myself before my turn to answer the GPA question. Because I'd failed pretty much everything, I was forced to change my major, and I lost every scholarship I'd worked so hard for. The message on repeat in my heart and mind? *I'm not enough.*

All the time spent in bed turned out to be the best thing that could've happened to me, because I was forced to sit alone with God and wrestle this whole thing out. I was completely aware of my inability to bring anything of value to the table, and I finally learned I didn't have to. With distractions of pride and accomplishment out of the way, He picked me up from my puddles of tears and shame, confirming this simple truth through prayer and scripture: I cannot earn His love, and I didn't need to try.

I'd love to say my identity struggle was settled in that dorm room amongst all the text books, pastel bedding, and plastic cutlery, but it wasn't. At least, not completely.

The broken part of us believes satisfaction comes when we are enough and when we have enough; so, we chase all kinds of things hoping to satisfy our thirsty souls. Those tiny sips of water work for a minute, but then they dry up, leaving us thirsty all over again. We might feel confused about why this keeps happening, but God isn't. He lays it out pretty clearly in Jeremiah:

My people have committed two sins:
They have forsaken me, the spring of living water,
and have dug their own cisterns,
broken cisterns that cannot hold water.[1]

Tired of being thirsty? There's only one well that never runs dry: Jesus.

In His words,[2] "If anyone is thirsty, let him come to me and drink. Whoever believes in me, as the Scripture has said, streams of living water will flow from within him." As our creator, Jesus is the only qualified source to satisfy our cravings. Nothing else is strong enough or big enough or lasting enough to bear the weight of our identity. He doesn't just quench our thirst; His never-ending supply fills us up and overflows into our parched and desperate world.

Friend, our identity has already been settled. Our identity isn't named by our achievements or what we lack; it's named by how God created us. How He sees us. He calls us:

A Masterpiece
Children of God
Friends
Accepted
Beloved

When our identity is in Christ, it's steadfast, secure, and unchanging. Nothing can alter it. Nothing else determines it. Not even you.

SCRIPTURE

Ephesians 2:1-10; Psalm 139:1-18

REFLECTION

1. When you look back on your life, what have you pursued to satisfy your soul's cravings?

Work, money/security, GF

2. How is Jesus better? (If you aren't sure that He is, be honest about that.)

He is true security, He never changes.

3. Look at Ephesians 2:10. Write or doodle it here.

For we are his workmanship created in Christ Jesus for good works which God prepared beforehand that we should walk in them.

TODAY'S PRAYER

Thank you that you don't change
and because of that I can be
grounded in you

PRACTICE

Draw an arrow pointing to the right. To the left
of the arrow, list the areas of your life where
you are believing, "I'm not enough." On the
right side of the arrow, write in big, bold,
letters: JESUS IS ENOUGH.

I'm not enough ⟶ Jesus is enough

Our Calling

"All of God's people are ordinary
people who have been made
extraordinary by the purpose
He has given them."
- *Oswald Chambers*

I grew up in a family with six Southern Baptist pastors. Just let your imagination run wild with that for a second. Six pastors in one family is a lot by anyone's standard, and as you can imagine, the whole dynamic produced some pretty entertaining conversations around the Thanksgiving table, but it also built an incredible legacy. Some had a history of missions and church planting before my lifetime, a few became missionaries during my childhood years, and others are still serving in pastoral roles now. Needless to say, from the time I was born, I was immersed in hymns, sermons, and Christian vernacular. When my little childhood friends and I played wedding, I was almost always the preacher, because I could perform an entire wedding ceremony from memory by the time I was six. Sometimes I was the bride and the preacher, because you can do that when you are playing pretend.

With all the daily Jesus-talk and countless hours sitting in the front row listening to my Daddy preach, it didn't take long for me to catch on to the idea that God has this super serious thing known as "a calling" for my life. However, major confusion lead me to two big misunderstandings: 1) God's calling was directly linked to a specific life-long vocation, and 2) I needed to have it figured out by age twenty (at the latest). Why age twenty? Who knows. It was some self-imposed deadline that sounded reasonable at the time. My twentieth birthday came and went, and I felt like my calling was doomed to remain a mystery forever—or worse, perhaps I was skipped when God passed them out.

Maybe you can relate.

We've made this idea of a calling mystical and complicated, almost as if our value hinges on finding it. We aren't exactly sure what we are looking for, but we're pretty sure it's unique and very impressive. We want to be significant. We want to be obedient. We want to do the right thing. And heaven forbid we make a wrong turn along the way.

I've met a lot of friends, both young and old, suffocating from the angst and pressure of figuring it all out. Does God have specific work for us to do? Yes (and we will talk more about that soon), but if we aren't careful, trying to figure out the right decisions, the right relationships, the right move to make, and the right career can so consume our attention, we miss the bigger picture. It's easy to focus on what hasn't been revealed yet when there's actually plenty that has. So, while we wait for specific instructions for our daily lives and futures, let's work on mastering what God has clearly revealed.

Here's the truth: Scripture presents a pretty simple framework for our calling as Christ-followers, and it has nothing to do with a job title. In fact, there's no finding "it" because it has everything to do with God finding us. You want to know your calling? You are called to belong to Christ through salvation, you are called to love God and people, and you are called to make disciples. If you survey the New Testament, you'll find a variety of terminology and analogies related to calling, but they all lead back to these three central themes.[1] My favorite analogy comes from Jesus in John 15, where He explains we've been chosen and appointed to bear an abundance of fruit; not just any fruit, fruit that lasts, that never spoils or decays.[2] God wants to make us increasingly effective in producing bountiful harvests of enduring fruit. He longs to enable us to do what we cannot do on our own - to love in ways we couldn't otherwise, to say yes to what's seemingly impossible, to shine God's light in a dark and hurting world in ways that point many to Jesus.

SCRIPTURE

John 15:1-17; Matthew 28:18-20;
2 Corinthians 5:16-21

REFLECTION

1. How do you think being a good steward of your life and bearing an abundance of fruit are connected?

_____

_____

_____

2. When you read Jesus' command to "go, therefore, and make disciples," what do you think that looks like in your life?

_____

_____

_____

3. Look up John 15:8 and write it below.

_____

_____

_____

TODAY'S PRAYER

_____

_____

_____

PRACTICE

List the names of one or two people who invested time in teaching you about Jesus. How
did you feel when you were with them? Write
them a note, text, or email to express what
they mean to you.

_____

_____

_____

_____

_____

_____

_____

Your Calling

> "If you read history, you will find that the Christians who did the most for the present world were precisely those who thought most of the next. It is since Christians have largely ceased to think of the other world, that they have become so ineffective in this."
> - *C.S. Lewis*

Have you ever reached the end of one of those non-stop days only to look back, shaking your head as you wonder, "What in the world did I do all day?" Yesterday was one of those days for me. Every moment was packed with "super important" meetings and busyness, but at the end, I felt as though I'd pretty much accomplished nothing. While it's not my favorite, I can be okay with a seemingly unproductive day from time-to-time, but I don't want to feel that way about my life as a whole. I bet you don't either. Have you ever wondered why we find those crazy-busy, yet oh-so-unproductive, days incredibly frustrating? Or what about the other extreme — why aren't we satisfied with laziness? Why is wasting too much time so bothersome? Sure, there's an element of responsibility moving us toward productivity, and personality certainly plays a role, but I think it stems from a much deeper, simpler truth: God created us to do stuff.

Not only are you called to belong to Christ through salvation, called to love God and people, and called to make disciples, God actually has specific work for you to do. We aren't just buying time until heaven; we have purpose here. Ephesians says you are God's masterpiece, "created in Christ Jesus to do good works, which God prepared in advance for us to do."[1] In other words, God uniquely created you with gifts, talents, and interests to serve the world you live in, and He has some specific ground-level work in mind for you to do. Friend, hear me on this: no one else can do your part. While this whole idea is exciting, humbling, and motivating, it can also feel a tad overwhelming at times. Here are three good things to keep in mind when it comes to your calling:

1. Your calling is continually in process. It's not something you can figure out by a certain age, and then maintain the rest of your life. To assume we should have God's complete purpose for our lives charted out by age twenty-five, thirty, or even fifty sets us up for failure, disappointment, and boredom. God is consistently developing us, stretching us, and shaping us for new seasons and assignments. Wherever you are in your life, there's more to come.

2. Assignments change. Our lives aren't stagnant — they are dynamic and changing. Some assignments may be life-long, but many won't. Be faithful and content with what's in front of you. Be all in and fully present, but still hold it all loosely. Don't become so attached to the here and now that you can't embrace change. Don't fix your feet in concrete. Keep pressing forward, stay flexible and ready to obey God, even when the next step leads right into unfamiliar and uncomfortable territory.

3. You won't fulfill your calling by accident. If it was a sure thing, we wouldn't have needed so many reminders throughout scripture to fulfill God's calling. It requires focus, endurance, and self-discipline. It requires intentionality and persistence, and a lifestyle of pressing in to God's heart through scripture, prayer, and God-centered community.

Can God's calling be in the form of what we would consider a "big ask?" Sure. God called Moses to free the entire nation of Israel from slavery. God called Mary to mother the Messiah. God called Paul to take the Gospel into hostile and life-threatening territory so the gentiles could be saved. Sometimes God calls people to start nonprofits, or to become a teacher, or to move to a new city, or a new country. All those scenarios have one thing in common: they didn't happen overnight. A lot of preparation and groundwork had to be in place before go-time. When we live fully surrendered to Christ, seasons of our lives tend to build on each other, which means God not only has work for you today, He is preparing you for what's to come. Do the dreams and desires God put in your heart feel far away or impossible? Don't lose heart. Start cultivating the skills and knowledge required to move them into fruition someday. Share them with trusted truth-tellers in your life, and pray about them often, trusting

God hears you, knows you, and holds your future.

God's calling isn't just reserved for "big asks." It's a good thing too, because our day-to-day lives would be confined to monotonous boredom otherwise. Instead, He offers tremendous purpose in the mundane. God's calling often feels pretty ordinary and looks a lot like you putting your unique gifts, talents, and interests to work. Look for whatever opportunities or needs are right in front of you, and get to it.

What are you waiting for?

SCRIPTURE

Acts 17:24-28; 1 Peter 4:7-11;
1 Corinthians 12:12-20

REFLECTION

1. What are the gifts, interests, talents, or abilities God has given you? Remember, they come in many forms.

_____

_____

_____

2. How can you put your gifts, talents, and interests to use for God's purpose in your office, your neighborhood, at your child's school, or in your church?

_____

_____

_____

3. What dream or desire has God placed in your heart? If you had to choose one way to start preparing for it, what would it be?

_____

_____

_____

4. Write or illustrate 1 Peter 4:10.

_____

_____

_____

TODAY'S PRAYER

_____

_____

_____

PRACTICE

Invite a friend out for coffee or over to your house for a conversation. Ask them to share one of their dreams with you. Then, help that person identify one step they can take toward their dream. Jot down who you are inviting and when you are planning to meet.

Comparison

"No one can make you feel inferior
without your consent."
- *Eleanor Roosevelt*

I had a long, un-enjoyable relationship with a Noisy Roommate. So much so, I not-so-affectionately call her "N.R." for short. I'm not talking about the kind of roommate who leaves dirty dishes in the sink and blares loud music until all hours of the night. I'm talking about the annoying voice in my head. Before you back away slowly from this book, or call my husband to express concern over me hearing voices, stick with me for a minute because you have one too. I'm talking about the voice that sounds a lot like yours, only it's accusing and negative rather than encouraging and truthful. It's the voice repeating messages like: *you aren't enough; you will fail; you aren't loved.*

Truth be told, I've learned to ignore her most of the time, but every now and then, something bumps the volume up a little too high. N.R.'s favorite storyline for the last decade can be summed up in one word: comparison. All sorts of scenarios initiate these one-sided conversations.

Heads turn as someone attractive walks in the room.
A smarter, more articulate colleague starts gaining the boss' attention in meetings.
That mom of a 4-month-old has a flatter tummy than I've ever even dreamed of.
That person hasn't worked half as long as I have to obtain _____, and yet they've got so much more.

My earliest memory of comparison is from when I was six. I woke up to my mother's usual, happy "Good Morning to You" song. I immediately burst into tears as she asked if I was ready for my first day of first grade. I spent every day of kindergarten admiring a first grader named Ashley. She was a head taller than everyone in her class and had a beautiful green dress that buttoned up the back with puffed sleeves and a ruffle just below the waist (thank you 80's fashion). She looked so beautiful and important, and *so first-grade*. Even though I was the tallest student in my class, I wasn't even close to Ashley's height. I didn't think I was tall enough for first grade, and I had no idea what to do about it. If it had been up to me, I would have just skipped first grade all together and stayed home, hidden beneath my blankets and stuffed animals. Thankfully, my mother quietly explained the truth as she held me: God made me the perfect size for me, and I was just right for first grade. Turns out, my mother was right. None of us needed to be as tall as Ashley to have great fun and achieve first grade success.

I can't say for sure, but I'm pretty convinced the destructive spiral of comparing ourselves to each another is one of the enemy's favorite tactics for compromising our impact, effectiveness, and joy. Before we know it, we are trapped in a spiral of discouragement and unmerited shame. Really, it boils down to this:

1. **Comparison keeps us from saying, "Yes!"** Whether it's "Yes" to a new friend, or "Yes" to a new opportunity, comparison robs us of more than we can even comprehend.

2. **Comparison distracts us.** Loving well is impossible when our thoughts are consumed by sizing up the competition.

The temptation to look from side to side at what others have isn't from God. Don't fall for it. God marked a lane for you to run in and you are just right for it. That N.R. is a dream killer and her weapon is comparison. Hang on to those God-dreams and desires for dear life and say a bold, "Yes" when opportunities to step up come. No one else has the same personality, gifts, passions, and abilities as you, so don't let comparison diminish your value or your dreams.

Friend, let's do this differently. What if we replace comparison with celebration? Instead of wishing for someone else's gifts, success, or abilities, let's celebrate who they are, how God made them, and the privilege we all share in being part of God's bigger story.

Let's believe and put on repeat: You are more than enough just as you are, because He is enough.

Let's be brave and humble and strong, because He is.

SCRIPTURE

Hebrews 2:1-3; Ephesians 3:14-21

REFLECTION

1. What situations kick up the volume on your N.R.?

Some one I think I'm better than has
more than ~~I~~ I do

2. Describe a time or two when comparison robbed you of joy or an opportunity.

DJ getting stuff,

TODAY'S PRAYER

Help me to find my acceptance
in you

PRACTICE

Write the portion of Galatians 5:25-26 that resonates most on a sticky note and place it on your bathroom mirror where you will see it every day.

———————————————

Since this is the kind of life we have chosen, the life of the Spirit, let us make sure that we do not just hold it as an idea in our heads or a sentiment in our hearts, but work out its implications in every detail of our lives. That means we will not compare ourselves with each other as if one of us were better and another worse. We have far more interesting things to do with our lives.
Each of us is an original.

Galatians 5:25-26 MSG

Balance

*"How we spend our days is of course
how we spend our lives."*
- Annie Dillard

If you've ever felt like you are drowning in your life, you are not alone. Sometimes, I look at my calendar and laugh. And of course, there's plenty that never actually makes it on my calendar, like my husband's entire world, feeding all the people who live under our roof, and kindergarten homework. (Can we take a moment to acknowledge how unprepared I was for kindergarten homework?) The question I receive more than any other is, "How do you do it all? As a mom, an executive, and a pastor's wife?" I'm pretty sure most of us are in the same boat, trying to put more in a day than should reasonably fit. Some of our busyness is absolutely necessary, no argument there, but some of it really isn't.

I recently had the privilege of facilitating a Bible study for a handful of teenage girls. When I asked what it takes to be a successful woman, it didn't take long to cover a flip chart page with their ideas: have a successful career, marry your soul mate, make a lot of money, own a home, be involved in the community, have kids who wear matching outfits (I know...I'm not kidding), drive a nice car, go to church, cook dinner every night, graduate from college. There was more, but you get the idea. I asked if anyone else was exhausted just looking at the list, and every single person raised their hand.

We laugh at the idea of actually achieving all of these "goals," but if we're honest, we have our own grown-up version of burdensome expectations. On one hand, we want to have it all (right now), and our overstuffed calendars and distracted hearts bear the evidence. On the other hand, we want balance, some reprieve - dare I say it? - permission to not have it all.

Here's what I'm learning: maintaining balance is a never-ending process because seasons change, needs change, and what requires our attention most changes. Just as building physical balance and endurance is difficult and uncomfortable (strange yoga pose anyone?), so is building life balance. It stretches us, causes us to grow, and it even feels a bit like work—because it is. A calm equilibrium is an illusion, and holding out for a picture-perfect reality ramps up the pressure and positions us for disappointment. The tension will always exist because our lives will never be stagnant. We were created for movement. If you are living on mission and on purpose, if you are using the gifts and talents God has given you, and if you are actively engaged in building His kingdom, your life will have plenty of meaningful activity.

There's often a disconnect between what we say our priorities are and where we spend our time. Balance is about aligning our priorities with our attention.

Though it may be a tough truth to swallow, having too many priorities is the same as having no priorities. Balance is not about giving everything equal time. Balance is about giving the right things the right amount of attention at the right time.

SCRIPTURE

Ephesians 5:1-17; Joshua 1:8

REFLECTION

1. What area of your life tends to be neglected? What would thriving in that area look like?

_____

_____

_____

2. Think about your career, physical health, family and relationships, and spiritual health. What does God really want for you in those areas?

_____

_____

_____

TODAY'S PRAYER

_____

_____

_____

PRACTICE

What is most important to you? (list no more than 5)

_____

_____

_____

_____

What can you say NO to, in order to say YES to what's most important?

_____

_____

_____

What's the risk in saying no to these things?

_____

_____

_____

_____

Is it worth the risk?

Yes ☐   **No** ☐   **Not Sure** ☐

Prayer

"By inventing the phenomenon of human prayer, God has decided to allow our asking to make a difference in the world."

- Gary Haugen

There's a huge, towering oak tree behind our home with branches covering most of our backyard. Because it leans a little too close to our garage for my comfort, I asked an expert to inspect the tree to make sure it wasn't going to topple over. He assured me the tree wasn't going anywhere because its roots go down deep, and it's far stronger than it appears. Just as the long-term greatness of a tree is found in the depth and health of its roots, so it is with us. Intimacy with God causes our roots to sink down deep, and without it, we cannot grow or bear fruit. Greatness doesn't begin with accomplishments and accolades, it begins underground. In secret. Through prayer.

One of my favorite Jesus moments is when He pulls a kiddo in front of an adult crowd to remind them that being adult isn't the end game here.[1] In fact, growing up can give us a false sense of confidence and of having things figured out. According to Jesus, the kids have it right: they don't have it all figured out, and they really don't have much to offer; they just believe in Jesus and want to be close to Him. Scripture calls us to active, authentic, substantial prayer lives, where true, original conversations flow straight from our hearts to God's, and from His heart to ours. But, it starts with a humble, needy, childlike faith positioning us before our Creator, fully recognizing everything of worth and value, and that everything our hearts and lives need, is found in Him alone.

Prayer is so much more than a discipline. Discipline can be a starting place, and even a valuable tool, but to reduce prayer to a mere discipline is to miss its power completely. We often approach prayer as just another box to check, but it's far more than an obligation.

Prayer is how we root our lives in what is true and real.

Prayer places God in a higher place of importance than our circumstances.

Prayer acknowledges our true dependence on God.

Prayer is how we overcome strongholds and wage war against the enemy.

Prayer cultivates subtle growth, and a fresh hunger for God.

Our tendency is to do everything but pray. We want to do something more "substantial," or we assume because consistent prayer doesn't come easily, we must not be cut out for it like others are. It feels easier to call a friend or to even go to church than to pray. Making a plan or trying to figure things out on our own can feel more productive than prayer. It's easier to fill our days with activities and work than it is to carve out time to pray. I've found myself in seasons where I didn't think I had time to pray, but nothing was further from the truth. Everything changes when we realize prayer is the most important work, and that we are completely hopeless to live victorious lives without building a strong foundation of prayer.

Prayer often occurs in unseen, unscripted moments. No one else may know if you curl up with your journal in your favorite chair to spend time with God before the household wakes up. No one else may notice if you slip into an empty room to whisper desperate pleas for wisdom before facilitating an intense meeting. No one may ever hear you pour out pain over death or loss or rejection before your head lands on the pillow for the night. God knows and He will see because He is with you in those moments. He fills up those spaces, and causes your roots to grow, sinking deep into the rich soil of His truth and grace.

Sometimes my prayer life has revolved around big things - salvation for a teenager, funding for a building, opportunities for ministry growth, or restoration of a friend's marriage. Some seasons have lead me to spend extended periods of time in prayer day after day. But on most days, I'm all about the small things, the opportunity to "pray without ceasing," as Paul writes.[2] *God, I'm exhausted by work and children and laundry. Would you lift me up and fill me with your strength? I have no idea what to say in this meeting. Would you give me your words? I'm at a loss on how to approach this project. Would you give me insight? I feel incredibly blah today. Would you fill my heart with joy and purpose?*

Jesus - the embodiment of God in the flesh - set aside time to talk with God often.

And rising very early in the morning, while it was still dark, he departed and went out to a desolate place, and there he prayed.[3]

But Jesus often withdrew to lonely places and prayed.[4]

In the days of his flesh, Jesus offered up prayers and supplications, with loud cries and tears, to him who was able to save him from death, and he was heard because of his reverence.[5]

If Christ sought solitary times of intimacy with the Father, how much more should we? Let's follow Jesus' example of being closely tied to God.

SCRIPTURE

Psalm 142:1-2; Phillippians 4:4-7;
Psalm 18:31-35; James 5:16

REFLECTION

1. How have you most recently been trying to culti-
vate growth in your spiritual life? (circle all that apply)

Trying to do the right things every day

✓ Intimacy with God through prayer

Keeping rules

✓ Reading scriptiure

I haven't really been intentional

2. What would it look like for prayer to become
even more foundational in your life?

Be more real and passionate

TODAY'S PRAYER

May I be more passionate in my
relationship and interaction with
you

PRACTICE

Praying God's Word is an incredible way to connect to God's heart and to the power of His Word. Choose one of the passages listed above to pray back to God using your own words.

_____

_____

_____

_____

_____

_____

_____

Humility

"Humble voices carry."
- Bob Goff

Humility has somehow grown to have a negative connotation. It's often mistaken for being weak or spineless, when it's quite the opposite. A humble leader has noble character and quiet strength. I feel like we need to set the record straight before we go one sentence further: low self-esteem or a quiet temperament does not equal humility. Being hard on yourself doesn't make you humble, and being outspoken or comfortable in front of a crowd doesn't disqualify you from humility. In fact, nothing could be further from the truth. Beth Moore explains this beautifully:

Low self-esteem means, I see myself as low — not because God is great, but because I have so little value. Don't miss the paradox. When I recognize the greatness of God, I fall on my face before Him, but I also see myself in a new light. Because I am the loved creation of so great a Maker, I cannot help but be a person of great worth. Low self-esteem has noth-

ing to do with real humility. Pride is self-absorption, whether we're absorbed with how miserable we are or how wonderful we are.[1]

(I recommend reading the above paragraph more than once to really let it sink in. In fact, go ahead and underline what stands out to you most.)

Pride - however it presents itself - crowds out humility. Humility can only be present when the truth of Christ fills our hearts, motivations, thoughts, and attitudes. We don't have to fight for recognition or a place in line; we don't have to prove our power, worth, or even our uniqueness. When our identities are firmly anchored in the truth of who Christ is, and who we are because of Christ, we are free to approach every decision, conversation, criticism, relationship, or opportunity from a place of confident assurance.

Being humble isn't really something you are, it's more something you do. Scripture tells us to put on humility,[2] be clothed with humility,[3] and to walk with humility.[4] Scripture also points to the tremendous benefits of humility: God esteems and gives grace to the humble.[5] (Don't you think being esteemed by God Himself sounds like a pretty big deal?) The inward work of humility directly impacts our outward relationships with people and with God. The presence or absence of humility in our lives and leadership leaves lasting impressions long after we are gone. Humility builds loyalty and lifts others up.

Consider Jesus. He led with no airs or pretense. He wasn't afraid to say hard things when they needed to be said, and He was unapologetically focused on the mission He came to accomplish. Though He was never in the wrong, He didn't feel the need to defend Himself or address every critic. His leadership was gentle and aggressive at the same time. While we don't know for sure how the disciples felt about His leadership, evidence strongly points to them feeling loved, valued, challenged, and empowered because those men (except Judas of course) went on to establish the early church, dedicating their lives to spreading the Gospel. Many even died as martyrs. I can't help but think their outcomes would have been dramatically different if 1) Jesus wasn't the real Messiah, or 2) He was a jerk.

What does leadership without humility look like? Prideful leadership reeks of accusation, control, or even passivity, while humble leadership breathes a sense of welcoming. You know because you've experienced it. We all have. At one time or another, we've served under leaders who lacked humility, and we've been the leader who lacked humility. We cannot change the past, but we certainly can redirect the future of our leadership by choosing humility.

Humble leaders don't get too far ahead. They patiently do what it takes to bring people with them.

Humble leaders make the hard calls when necessary. Their quiet strength creates safety and energizes those they lead.

Humble leaders use their position as a platform for service. Their goal is to call out the best in others. They approach leadership from the perspective of serving rather than being served.

If you want the ripple effects of your leadership to be long-lasting and impactful, if you want the eyes of those you lead to shine with confidence and possibility, and if you want to focus on what's most important, humility is the way.

SCRIPTURE

Philippians 2:3; Proverbs 22:4; Colossians 3:12

REFLECTION

1. Colossians 3:12 tells us to cloth ourselves with humility. What does it looks like to wear humility?

We would be kind without expecting return

2. How does humility change our response when we feel overlooked, under-appreciated or misunderstood?

gives us true perspective

TODAY'S PRAYER

Decrease me Lord

PRACTICE

In 1 Peter 5:1-11, Paul is explaining humble leadership to elders in the early church. They were responsible for leading and overseeing the local church through teaching, encouraging and correcting, guarding against false teaching, and caring for their needs.[6] Your leadership role may not be that of an elder in a local church, but this passage paints a vivid picture of how you should lead. Read 1 Peter 5:1-11 and list the characteristics of Godly leadership you find.

oversight   not compulsion   willing
good example   humbles   sober

What does verse 10 describe as the benefit of leading this way?

eternal glory

Who do you know that embodies humble leadership?

Moody, Nat, Drew, Michael Borsman

Faith

"How glorious the splendor of a
human heart that trusts that it is loved."
- *Brennan Manning*

We want people to believe us. It even bothers us and hurts our feelings when people don't - especially when they know us. Why? Because our words mean something to us, and we mean what we say. Disbelief creates distance and distrust, and no relationship of any sort can deepen without trust, including our relationship with God. We say with our mouths that we trust Him, but do we really? Do our lives, behaviors, and thoughts really line up with our words?

I used to think faith was about believing in God, but now I know faith is much more about *believing* God.

In my lifetime, I've had the privilege of observing a handful of Faith Giants - individuals whose faith is alive, active, and bold. They live hundreds of miles apart, vary in age and ethnicity, and align with a wide spectrum of denominational leanings. Though strangers to one another, they have more in common than they will ever know. They pray with confidence for things that seem impossible. When circumstances are overwhelming and chaotic, they are steady. They wholeheartedly believe God is who He says He is, and that they are as loved, redeemed, and empowered as He says they are. They actually believe in the abilities and promises of God, and they stake their lives on them. It's no surprise their dynamic faith continues to call me out, making me want to believe God more today than I did yesterday.

There's a dramatic difference between believing in God and believing God. Some of us exercise faith at salvation, but don't take it much further. Before we realize what's happening, living with autopilot faith becomes the norm. It's as if we are afraid to put Him on the spot. We trust Him with our eternal destination, but not much else, so we start putting limitations on what we ask and pray for, so we won't be disappointed. Scripture makes a bold claim: without faith it's impossible to please God.[1] This sounds like a harsh truth, but it's really the basic, simple foundation of a real relationship with God. Keep in mind, faith isn't merely an action, it's the most natural response to understanding and experiencing the faithfulness of God.

Seasoned and established faith grows and builds over time. It comes from pouring over scripture and rubbing shoulders with other believers who are at different stages in their journeys. It's strengthened when we reach the end of our abilities and resources and God does the impossible right before our very eyes. It's encouraged when the nearness of God is almost as tangible as the air we breathe. It's solidified when we learn to trust God even when the outcomes don't match our desires, or when we can't see or feel Him at all.

Fear is the enemy of faith. I don't know about you, but fear tends to creep in most when I feel out of control, stressed, or overwhelmed. Sometimes fear feels a lot like worry over a hard decision, or anxiety as I play potential outcomes over and over in my mind. Regardless of the label, it's all fear. You might recall the story from Mark 4 where Jesus' disciples panicked as a raging storm filled their boat with water while Jesus slept.[2] They woke Jesus up with a question we can all identify with: "What are you doing? Don't you care about us?" Jesus commanded the storm to cease with just a few words. Of course, He did. He was in complete control of the sea and always had been — from the day He spoke the sea into existence all the way to that terrifying day in the boat. The question He asked His disciples was the one He still asks us today, "Why are you so afraid? Do you still have no faith?"[3] Their fear left no room for faith, even though Jesus was right there with them the whole time.

He's with us too, and He is in control.
He always has been.

Almost a decade ago, my friend Leah asked me what I wanted for Christmas. I jokingly replied, "Faith!" I played it off as kidding, but I was facing some big decisions and even bigger needs. I knew God was pulling me forward into His plans, but I felt like I was blindly jumping off a cliff. There was nothing logical about it, the timing seemed horrible, and I couldn't see how in the world all the details would come together. When Christmas rolled around, I checked the mailbox and found a gift from Leah: a black and white box with a green lid full of tiny rolled up pieces of paper, each one with a scripture or simple truth about God, faith, or what it means to believe God. I choked back tears as I called to say thank you. She sweetly explained, "Meredith, you asked for faith, so I'm giving you a box of faith. When yours runs out, take a truth from this box and let it be a reminder God has all you need."

That box holds a place of honor in my office to this day, and when my faith feels shaky, I open the box, pull out one of those tangible reminders of God's power, and confess all my fear to Him as I ask Him to help my unbelief. And slowly but surely, my faith continues to grow.

Yours can too.

SCRIPTURE

Romans 10:17; Ephesians 1:18-21;
Isiah 43:10; Hebrews 11:6

REFLECTION

1. How would you describe the difference between believing in God and believing God?

accept His Words as fact

2. What stirs up your faith? (Studying scripture, prayer, spending time with certain people, etc.?)

Jesus working

3. How would faith coming more alive in your heart impact your thoughts and decisions?

More bold and Christ centered

TODAY'S PRAYER

Help my unbelif

PRACTICE

1. Read Mark 9:14-24

2. What did the boy's father say in verse 24?

Help my unbelif

3. List the areas of your life where you are struggling with unbelief, then confess them to God, asking Him to help your unbelief.

You are my power

Wisdom

"Get the truth and never sell it; also get wisdom, discipline, and good judgement."
-*Proverbs 23:23 (NLT)*

I remember begging God for wisdom before I drifted off to sleep one night. Well, there have been many of those nights, but this one in particular stands out in my mind because I was at a complete loss on how to handle the situation I would face the next day. When I woke in the morning, the same prayer was on my mind, "God, please help me! I need wisdom to know what to do!" Hard conversations were waiting for me at the office, and being in charge felt like more than I'd signed up for. I went into the meeting with one plan, but the Holy Spirit intervened, and the conversation went in the opposite direction, which turned out to be the right direction. Thank goodness for divine intervention and the power of the Holy Spirit to lead us when we don't know what to do, what to say, or where to go.

This whole leadership journey - both personally and professionally - has made James 1:5[1] an almost daily prayer for me.

If any of you lacks wisdom, you should ask God, who gives generously to all without criticizing, and it will be given to him.

The complexities of our lives leave plenty of questions to be answered. What should we do about childcare, our job, or our marriage? Some of us are facing financial trouble, and we aren't sure what to do. We have friends who are drowning in depression, and we don't know how to love them well. Our bodies are betraying us with health concerns, and we don't know what treatment plan is best. Our businesses are struggling, gossip is spreading, and we don't know how to stop it. A recent promotion is bringing new responsibilities that are far outside our comfort zone, and we have no clue where to start. We need practical advice for the here and now, because not every detail of every decision can be found in scripture.

We are invited to ask God for as much wisdom as we need, as often as we need. While we may tend to beat ourselves up for lacking the wisdom to make decisions on our own, He will never scold us for our lack, and He isn't stingy with His wisdom either. He delights in pouring it out in abundance! It's such a beautiful promise.

It's tempting to go to people for wisdom instead of God. Yes, God certainly uses people to guide us in His ways, but scripture is pretty clear. We need to ask Him. And when we do, we can be assured what we are sensing is truly from God if it bears the marks and characteristics of Godly wisdom. "But the wisdom from above is first pure, then peace-loving, gentle, compliant, full of mercy and good fruits, without favoritism and hypocrisy."[2] The world's wisdom is characterized by envy, selfish ambition, and disorder.[3] It's harsh and hasty. If you line up Godly wisdom next to worldly wisdom, it's not difficult to see how the outcomes will vary, and so much is determined by the true motivations of our hearts.

SCRIPTURE

James 1:1-8; James 3:13-18; Proverbs 4:6-7

REFLECTION

1. Who do you personally know that you would characterize as having Godly wisdom?

_____

_____

_____

_____

_____

_____

2. Where do you need wisdom in your life right now?

_____

_____

_____

_____

_____

TODAY'S PRAYER

_____

_____

_____

PRACTICE

Set a daily reminder to ask God for wisdom for the next 10 days and journal about your experience. Write the time of your reminder below.

Bravery

"Farmers who wait for perfect weather never plant. If they watch every cloud, they will never harvest."
- Ecclesiastes 11:4 (NLT)

I had an irrational fear of the dark as a little girl. Not all the time, just mostly when I spent the night at my grandmother's. I have no idea why, because absolutely nothing ever happened there to make me feel afraid. In fact, some of my happiest childhood memories were created there, but when bedtime came, and the house went dark, I became afraid. No rationalization or nightlight could dispel my fear. I eventually grew out of it, and though it seems silly now, it was very real at the time. Adult fears are just as real.

Before we know it, fear can make itself a little too much at home.

Fear of having hard conversations.
Fear of taking risks.
Fear of letting others down.
Fear of failing.
Fear of making the wrong decision.
Fear of rejection.

Fear of what others think.
Fear of not being enough.

Even the disciples were well acquainted with fear, and we see it on broad display in Luke 9. After hours of Jesus teaching the multitudes, tummies started to rumble with hunger. Rather than sending the crowds away to find dinner, Jesus looked at the disciples and said, "You give them something to eat."[1] While scripture doesn't exactly say, I can only imagine fear gripped their hearts. They didn't have enough food, they didn't have enough money, and there was nothing they could do about it. With the pressure (and hunger) mounting, Jesus stepped in and miraculously fed more than 5,000 people with five loaves and two fish. Jesus was right there with them, and they'd seen Him do miracles before, yet they still felt confined by their own logic and understanding. When I read this story, the lesson isn't so much about hungry people being fed. It's about fearful, doubting disciples being reminded of God's infinite power and resources.

Fear kicks in when our human understanding cannot reconcile our circumstances. When things don't make sense, or they feel too big or too hard, or the risk seems too great. When we can't seem to conjure up the answers or resources, the door swings wide for fear to walk in and make itself at home. I struggled with admitting fear to God and to others for decades because scripture is full of reminders to not be afraid; so, I thought there was something wrong with me. I didn't understand faith and fear can co-exist. Scripture is full of weak, unqualified, terrified people used to accomplish amazing feats because God was with them, and He used them in spite of their fear. Yes, we have been set free from the burden of fear, but like so many other areas, learning to walk in that freedom is a life-long process.

What if we quit letting fear hold us back? What if we quit waiting for it to disappear before we make a move? Fear itself isn't the biggest issue; what we do with our fear matters most. We are humans with limited knowledge, and our line of sight only goes so far. We only know what we know, and we often have more questions than answers. But, what are we actually doing with our fear? Are we naming it or ignoring it? Are we hiding it or handing it over to the one who knows our future?

There's something about the word "brave," isn't there? Go ahead. Say it outloud.

Brave.

It pulls on something deep inside. I recently watched my young daughter conquer a big fear. Afterward, I held her little face in my hands and said, "Sweetheart, you are so brave." That little five letter word invoked something in her too. Her eyes danced with pride and her smile couldn't have been any bigger as she stood up a little straighter and pushed her shoulders back. I want to be brave, and so do you. I think we'd all agree being brave is a good thing; in fact, it's something to celebrate. But, one thing we seem to forget: fear always precedes bravery. I don't think bravery is the absence of fear. I think you can be simultaneously afraid and brave. Bravery is simply refusing to let fear hold us back.

We spend a lot of energy trying to avoid scary things, but I think God wants something else from us. He wants us to be brave.

SCRIPTURE

Philippians 4:6-7; Matthew 13:1-23;
1 Timothy 1:7

REFLECTION

1. Where has fear made itself at home in your heart?

_____

_____

_____

_____

_____

_____

2. When have you previously pressed on in spite of fear?

_____

_____

_____

_____

_____

TODAY'S PRAYER

_____

_____

_____

PRACTICE

Take a few minutes to sketch out your own "Bradge of Bravery." (Be sure to put your name on it!)

Multiplication

"The value of a life is largely determined by how much has
been given away."
- *Andy Stanley*

If you think about it, our time here on earth is really short. The older we get, the more time passes at lightning speed. And when you begin to appreciate how quickly time goes, you can't help but consider how you're living your life. Are you making the most of your time? Are you living on purpose? Are you investing in others? Are you building a legacy?

From Genesis to Revelation, scripture breathes multiplication. From the foundation of the world, God's plan for his kingdom—for his people, for us—is multiplication. Yes, God tells Adam and Eve to be fruitful and multiply by having children, but it's so much more. When God created man and woman, the crown of all His creation, He stamped them with His image. God's command to multiply was very much about taking the image of God, and His rule and reign, and spreading it all over the earth. Throughout the old testament, we see God's people repeating the cycle of rebellion, slavery, and repentance. However, just because mankind sins, God's plan for the multiplication of His image and His glory doesn't stop. His people never stopped multiplying, and in the New Testament, Jesus echoed this theme through parables and stories. Jesus' final instructions before ascending into heaven emphasized multiplication, but this time, the charge was, "Go make disciples."[1] Regardless of what else fills our time and holds our attention, we're to be making disciples.

The popularity of "giving back" is a major pro in our culture right now. You can shop with purpose for almost anything, and donations pour in after natural disasters. As I'm writing, my community isn't far removed from catastrophic flooding due to a hurricane of unprecedented proportions. In the days and weeks immediately following the storm, people across our nation mobilized to send massive amounts of supplies and funds to help. It was truly an incredible outpouring of love. There's a lot of people doing a lot of good, a lot of causes being championed, but the temptation in this give back movement is believing a few "good things" sprinkled here and there are enough. Jesus didn't just set the bar higher, He created a whole new standard. Before Jesus, the old way of doing things had a lot to do with doing a lot of good to uphold the law. His new way - the best, most life-giving way - has a lot to do with sharing and investing our lives in others.

I can almost hear audible moans coming from your side of the pages, and if I had to guess, the reason is probably on this list:

1. You don't have time. Yes, it's important to scale back busyness so time matches the priorities we claim, but there's good news here regardless. Investing in others doesn't always require large blocks of time. In fact, it's often most effective to simply include others in our day-to-day lives. Connect over lunch (we all have to eat!) or invite someone to your child's soccer game. It could even be a monthly 45-minute phone call. Simplicity and consistency go pretty far.

2. You feel unqualified. "I'm disqualified because I'm not a model _____ (parent, leader, spouse, etc.)." Your life is like a treasure chest, full of wins and losses, successes and failures. Burying it doesn't do anyone any good. We assume everyone wants to hear stories of success, but in reality, they are mostly interested in stories of failure. After all, when we look back, didn't our failures shape us the most?

3. You don't know who to invest in. There's no formula, so don't fall prey to "paralysis of analysis." Lead a small group at your church, take a younger co-worker under your wing, read to elementary students on your lunch break, or mentor at-risk youth. If you are really stuck, look for someone currently navigating the stages you've completed. Get a name and a face in mind, then offer encouragement, pray for them, and invite them over for dinner.

Inevitably, we all need to cut some habits and obligations to make space for more of what multiplies. Let's cut out some Netflix, social media time, pointless meetings, and a few extracurriculars. Let's simplify, but as we do, let's make sure investing in other stays.

It is our responsibility and privilege to leverage our lives for those coming along behind. And if we don't, who will?

SCRIPTURE

2 Corinthians 9:6-8; Matthew 12:1-23

REFLECTION

1. What 3 things do you want people to say about your life when it comes to an end?

_____

_____

_____

_____

2. What 2 people (outside of your family) went above and beyond to invest in your life (personally, professionally, or spiritually) and what did you learn from them?

_____

_____

_____

_____

TODAY'S PRAYER

_____

_____

_____

PRACTICE

Brainstorm a list of people in your life who are currently navigating life stages you've completed. Choose on to reach out to with encouragement this week.

_____

_____

_____

_____

_____

_____

_____

Failure

> "The difference between average people and achieving people is their perception of and response to failure."
> *- John Maxwell*

Our family's daily morning exodus is quite a sight. There are only four of us, two of which are still quite small, but there's a ton of gear to carry, shoes to tie, and hugs and kisses to dish out. It's a jumbled mess, but we love it. Last year's first tease of fall made us unreasonably excited to step outside, especially because we live on the oppressively hot and humid Texas gulf coast—where cool weather is an exception to our year-round summer. The crisp air gave our not quite two-year-old Ella some extra energy, and when you are that small, enthusiasm and joy are best expressed through squeals and running in circles. The momentum of it all got the best of her and the circles ended with a double-knee-plant in the driveway.

As her look of shock turned to tears, her Daddy scooped her up as only a Daddy can. All at once, Abigail and I dropped the mounds of gear piled in our arms to join Daddy in pouring out comfort and kisses. David and I did what all parents do in these moments:

distracted her with cheerios and silly songs while cleaning the gravel from her bloody knees. As her tears dried, all our distraction shenanigans turned to cheers and affirmations for earning her FIRST Frozen Band-Aids - a major rite of passage for the King girls. The three of us huddled in close around Ella as we placed a prized Band-Aid on each knee. Abigail said it best (while clapping and literally jumping up and down - not a surprise if you know Abigail), "Ella! You got your first Frozen Band-Aids! We are so proud of you!"

But the best part was watching Ella's face. Her expression moved from pain to fear, from sadness to confusion, and finally to innocent pride. Somehow, in her own little way, she understood those Frozen Band-Aids represented more than just Olaf and Anna.

Oh, friends. When did we stop celebrating scraped knees and bruises? At what age do tumbles and missteps turn from the process of learning to fatal errors? When exactly does shame start to overshadow the joy of Frozen Band-Aids? When did we first believe making mistakes makes us a mistake?

I'm fully aware it's not as simple as a double-knee-plant in the driveway. Our bruises and scrapes are deeper, bigger, and last longer than a few moments. Sometimes those moments, those years, wound our souls. Sometimes they wound others. But where exactly is the dividing line between what God's grace is wide enough to cover and what it's not? Where does the opportunity for redemption and hope run out? Who decides what failure is small enough to come back from and what is just too big, too bad, too much? When did we start to believe we are the only ones with difficult stories and painful pasts, with moments we aren't proud of, with bruised souls and broken dreams? When did we decide those things disqualify us from belonging, from impacting the world, from having a seat at the table?

If only we could grow right into flawless lives, but much like a child learning to ride a bicycle, we are going to fall down sometimes. We will fail in relationships, in business, and in leadership, but the key is failing forward instead of becoming paralyzed by our failure. About the time we think we've got it together, we'll fail again. And again. And again. Failing means we are trying things, we are moving the needle on the dial, we are engaged and getting our hands dirty. The question to ask is, "What can I learn?" not, "Should I quit?"

In a world full of differences and agendas, our brokenness is the most common ground we have. When God finds us in all our tears and failures, He scoops us up like only a Daddy can, and He makes us brand new. And those heartbreaking moments, those devastating blows, those terrible decisions become stories of healing, redemption, and overcoming. Stories other broken people need to hear.

Please hear this. There are plenty of seats at His table, and it's not like there's one lonely chair at the far end for the broken person who slips in through the back door. No, no. The seats are only for broken people, for those well acquainted with failure.

SCRIPTURE

Proverbs 24:16; Psalm 40:1-3; Romans 8:1-11

REFLECTION

1. How has hearing others' stories of life's bruises, failures and brokenness encouraged you?

I don't celibrate that anymore

2. What failures have you allowed to define you, or at least caused you to hesitate in moving forward?

Basic

3. List the failures you are okay sharing with others.

forgetting stuff dad tells me
first semester at school
LA trip

4. List the failures you prefer to keep hidden.

lust
stuff with Ashley

Do you think God can redeem your failures?

Yes ☒   No ☐

TODAY'S PRAYER

Help me turn Failure into opertunity

PRACTICE

When thinking back on the failures you listed, what life-lessons did you learn?

personal resposibitiy

some things suck

Prep is very needed in my life

What types of people would be helped by knowing your failures and what you learned?

recruits?

sls?

Now find, someone who falls within one of the above categories and create an opportunity to share your story and experiences with them this week.

Write the name of the person you have in mind here.

Words

"O Lord, keep our hearts, keep our
eyes, keep our feet, and keep our
tongues."
- William Tiptaft

A few years ago, the staff from True To Life Ministries
ventured a few miles out of town for a retreat. We were
out in the middle of nowhere, a refreshing change of
scenery for all of us city-folk. After full days of praying
and planning and preparing for the future, the retreat
culminated with everyone gathering around the camp-
fire sharing stories and eating s'mores. And then, as
if directed by an unseen hand, we looked upward and
erupted into joyous awe: "THOSE STARS ARE AMAZ-
ING!" We'd seen the stars a thousand times, but out
there, surrounded by darkness, the stars were new.
The big, bold lights stood in stark contrast against the
velvety black sky. It was as if that moment connected
us to history - to the generations before who relied on
those same stars to see and to navigate. They were
bright beacons that could be counted on. They wer-
en't just beautiful, they were important, because they
helped guide people home.

We are supposed to be like those stars. Scripture

tells us the same God who created light to shine out of darkness turns His light on in our hearts, illuminating our need for Jesus and establishing His light in us to the point when we actually become His light. He holds us up and positions us to shine in our world — a world full of darkness, brokenness, and sin. Jesus charges us to take His light and shine it brightly — to become bold beacons of light pointing people to God and guiding them home. He even goes as far as saying, "You are the light of the world" — a city on a hill that cannot be hidden.[1] It's easy to say a passionate, "YES!" because we really do want our lives to shine brightly. We want to be different. We want to point people to Jesus. But how?

The how gets me every time.

Paul lays it out for us in Philippians 2: *Do everything without complaining or arguing, so that you may be blameless and pure, children of God who are faultless in a crooked and perverted generation, among whom you shine like stars in the world.*[2]

Want to know how to make our lives shine brightly? Do everything without complaining or arguing. It sounds so anticlimactic until you actually try to live it out in the real world and realize how hard it is.

I was recently the topic of some yucky gossip. While I don't think full-on malicious intent was behind it, it still hurt. It didn't even make me angry, it just left me kind of puzzled. I kept thinking, "Don't they have something better and truer to talk about?" It didn't take the Holy Spirit long to point that question inward toward my heart. He quietly whispered, "Meredith, what about your words? What are you talking about?"

Since then, I've been thinking a lot about the words

coming out of my mouth. Do they lift up or tear down? Do they point toward truth or foster negativity? Are they words of life or death? Do they leave people encouraged or frustrated? Do they make people feel included or alienated? Are they true, lovely, and worth repeating?

Sometime ago, I read a disturbing article explaining that 30-40% of our conversations are some version of complaining.[3] All sorts of defensiveness rose up in me, until I realized how true it actually was. Complaining is the language of our culture. It's how we strike up conversations, and how we find common ground. We greet the person in the coffee shop line by complaining about how hot (or cold) the weather is. We blast restaurants on social media for subpar food. We express frustration about slow drivers, slow internet, and slow customer service. We grumble and sigh about our workloads and stress levels when we get home, and we voice plenty of offense when others don't treat us the way we feel they should. We voice our annoyances over coffee dates, texts, or dinners with friends. It comes up at work and in our leisure time, in emails, in real conversations, and on our social media feeds.

Something from inside our hearts rises up in defense: "Well, I was annoyed/offended/disappointed! I'm allowed to voice my opinion, aren't I?" Yes. We are allowed, and the majority of us fully utilize our freedom; and when we do, we fit right in. But that's the whole point: we aren't supposed to fit it.

Especially as leaders, our words carry weight and influence. Mixing the praise of Jesus with cutting remarks doesn't make sense. The words we speak - especially to people and about people - either amplifies the message of Jesus or confuses it. Our words in unscripted moments tell the true story of our hearts. We don't just need behavior change, we need heart change. A genuine concern for Christ breeds genuine concern for people, and when our hearts are fixed on Christ and are intent on loving people, it will be reflected in our words and in our lives. Then we will shine brightly.

SCRIPTURE

Luke 6:43-45; Ephesians 4:29;
Proverbs 18:20-21

REFLECTION

1. What circumstances tempt you most to jump on the "complaining bandwagon?"

_____

_____

_____

2. As Christ-followers, what impact would avoiding "complaining or arguing" have in our relationships with unbelievers?

_____

_____

_____

3. Who do you know who maintains positive speech (no gossip, complaining, etc.)? How do you feel when you are around them?

_____

_____

_____

TODAY'S PRAYER

_____

_____

_____

PRACTICE

My Words:
(Choose all that apply)

- ☐ Lift up
- ☐ Tear down
- ☐ Inspire
- ☐ Discourage
- ☐ Are true
- ☐ Are empty

Because much of what we say comes directly from our hearts, let's make sure true, positive things are filling our hearts!

Keep a 10-day gratitude list on your phone or in your journal. List one thing you are grateful for each day. Be sure to bring up something you are grateful for from time-to-time in conversations.

Friendship

"You are those who have stood by
me in my trials."
- Luke 22:28

I'm certain you've been there too: in a crowded, loud
room, full of laughter and conversation, yet feeling
alone and deeply unknown. As leaders, we learn to
move with the rhythms of smooth interactions and
roles we are asked to play. With practice, we master
the art of conversation and listening, and we become
great sounding boards for others' dreams and ambi-
tions. Sometimes I think we confuse others knowing
our names with actually being known. However, our
hearts know the difference.

One of scripture's most beautiful displays of friendship (in my opinion) is found in Exodus 17 where the
Israelites are going into battle with the Amalekites.
After Moses sends Joshua to gather up men to fight,
he climbs to the top of a hill to stand with God's staff
in his hand. For some added context, keep in mind,
God made this staff do wondrous things in the past
- parting water for example - so the Israelites would
know God was with them and for them. Sure enough,

as Moses raised his staff, the Israelites prevailed over their enemy, but when Moses lowered the staff, the Israelites started to lose. Lowering the staff wasn't really an option, but Moses was old, and scripture tells us "his hands grew heavy."[1] Thankfully, Moses had the foresight to bring two friends with him. Aaron and Hur stepped in to help because there was no way Moses could keep his staff up in the air on his own. They found a stone for Moses to sit on, and then Aaron and Hur held up Moses' hands for him until the battle was over and God's people had won.

The Israelites needed God, and God made it so they needed Moses too. Even though Moses was a strong, proven leader, he needed Aaron and Hur, because he wasn't strong enough on his own. If we want to grow, if we want to be effective, if we want to run our races well, we need each other. It's a counter-cultural concept because pride has slipped into our hearts in unsuspecting ways to equate strength and confidence with not needing below-the-surface friendships. Many of us avoid vulnerability because we are terrified of what people would think if they knew who we really were—as if somehow, they would love, respect, or like us less.

I'm convinced we are all craving safe people right now, and it's not a new craving - God placed it in us at creation. If you start to doubt the importance of friendship, just look at scripture: Jesus had His disciples. David had Johnathan. Ruth had Naomi. Mary had Elizabeth. Paul had Timothy. Each of them loved God deeply, and they stood shoulder-to-shoulder, supporting each other, encouraging one another to trust God's plans and to live obediently. When I think back on my own story, God continues to use key people to shape my life, my faith, my character, and even my work. I could list a solid handful of people who have tremendously impacted my life, some of whom are still walking with me today. What if I'd missed out on those friendships? What if I withheld my heart, or what if they held back their lives? What if we hadn't invested the time required for building real friendships? We would have missed such value and beauty.

Previous relationships may be our biggest obstacles to our next relationships. "A relationship can either be so good we make no room for another or so bad we refuse to take a second risk."[2] It's tempting to keep everything surface-level and professional, instead of getting personal. It's easy to shut down after a falling out, or to buy the lie that says staying ahead means withholding our hearts. What is the cost to us and others when we don't lean in? After all, the whole idea of being created for friendship and community means we not only need real, true friends, they need us too.

While we do need friendship, we must be wise about who walks uphill with us. Moses was highly selective in choosing Aaron and Hur. Jesus chose only twelve men to share life on a deep, intimate level. As leaders, we can be friends with many people, and we can love a lot of people well, but when it comes down to it, we need a handful in our closest circle who are trustworthy, loving, loyal, and willing to tell us the truth. True community is found with people who are for us, void of personal agendas, and who aren't wrapped up in co-dependent tendencies. They encourage our faith and challenge us to move forward. They hold up our arms, and we hold up theirs.

SCRIPTURE

Proverbs 27:17; Hebrews 10:19-25;
Ecclesiastes 4:9-10; Proverbs 13:20

REFLECTION

1. Is your tendency to lean-in to friendships, or with-hold? How is your tendency impacting your faith? Your leadership?

_____

_____

_____

2. Who are your "uphill" friends?

_____

_____

3. Have you ever been in a friendship you knew was unhealthy? How did (or does) that friendship impact you?

_____

_____

4. What do you need to work on to become a better "uphill" friend for someone else?

_____

_____

TODAY'S PRAYER

_____

_____

_____

PRACTICE

Who could benefit from your vulnerability and willingness to help "hold up their arms?" Jot down their name and some ideas of what it would look like to do that for them. Call them or spend time with them in the next week.

Celebration

"Sometimes we become so focused
on the finish line that we fail to find joy
in the journey."
- *Dieter F. Uchtdorf*

I cannot explain the sheer volume of cupcakes our family consumes the first ninety days of the year, simply because all four of our birthdays fall between January and March. Our girls approach each cupcake feast with the same strategy: carefully inspect every cupcake, then choose the one with the most sprinkles. While I'm personally a cupcake purist - simple buttercream icing on vanilla cake is my favorite - I think the girls are on to something. Nothing says celebration like a cupcake covered in bright sprinkles; so in that regard, the more sprinkles the better.

Every party has a reason. We host birthday parties, Christmas parties, and dinner parties. We go to office parties and block parties. Our kids have tea parties. Parties are defining moments, and when the occasion is long past, we have the memories to look back on. My favorite party in the Bible is found in Luke 15 when Jesus tells the Parable of the Prodigal Son. The son leaves his father's home and squanders everything he was given, living in sin and darkness until his life hit the bottom. Instead of forgetting him or begrudging him, his father watched for his return in great anticipation. When he finally sees him coming, he runs to his son, embracing him and kissing him. He welcomes him with a party of all parties because his beloved son has finally come home. Can you imagine the hope, the extravagant love, and sense of belonging the son felt?

As a mother, I make a point to celebrate my daughters' accomplishments: first steps, first words, blue ribbons, learning to read, showing kindness to a friend, and even doing chores. But with an overflowing calendar and high drive for productivity, I'm not always quick to celebrate the milestones of those I lead, or of my own life, for that matter. It's even easier to breeze right by the smaller details, even though they are just as worthy of celebration and remembrance. There's a tiny rock on my office bookshelf from the trip to Canada I talked about in the introduction to this book. You might recall, I made the journey in brokenness and exhaustion. I still remember standing beside a crystal-clear mountain stream, the cold wind causing my eyes to sting and water as I breathed slow, deep breaths, whispering a quiet prayer under my breath for God to put my heart back together. And He did. I felt Him in that place, and I knew I wanted to remember God's nearness in that moment; so, I reached down and picked up a smooth, dark gray stone. I brought it home, and put it in a place of honor. Celebration is certainly expressed through parties and cute decorations, but that rock is its own kind of celebration - a little, tiny stone of remembrance because I don't want to forget God's faithfulness in my struggle.

Throughout the Bible, God asks us to remember, and I'm convinced it's because we are prone to forget. I can't help but think about when God led Joshua and the Israelites across the Jordan River on dry land as they entered the Promise Land (the second time God parted water for His people, mind you).[1] God flexed His power by making a way where there was no way, leaving no room for questions regarding His presence. Before the waters came back together, God told Joshua to choose twelve men to walk right back to the center of the Jordan where the priests stood with the ark of the covenant, and to each bring back a stone "to serve as a sign among you."[2] Joshua stacked up those stones as a marker - a reminder - of God's deliverance, so when their children asked about the stones, and when God's people were tempted to forget what He had done, they had a tangible reminder of God's story.

One of the most tangible ways I remember who God has been to me is looking through my shelf full of journals going back to my college days. Page after page records joys and sorrows, scriptures, prayers, and milestones. When I read them, I look back with confidence, knowing God hears me because I see those same events through the perspective of time, maturity, and answered prayer. Remembering what God has done builds my faith and inspires hope when my circumstances or emotions cause me to doubt.

Celebrations bring a sense of belonging and gratitude. They mark what's important, and they help us remember. God wants us to remember the events, people, and places that point us to Him. The more intentional we are, the more we will find to celebrate. Celebration cultivates gratitude in us because in some form or fashion, every celebration is fueled by gratitude. So, if you've been praying about something, and one morning God clearly answers your prayer through scripture, write it down. When a friend encourages you, or when you achieve something special, stack up a few stones. When God hears your silent prayers, or proves His love to you in some sort of tangible way, grab the sprinkles!

SCRIPTURE

1 Chronicles 16:8-13; Psalm 105:1-5

REFLECTION

1. When you think of personal milestones you've accomplished, what's been your favorite?

_____

_____

_____

_____

_____

2. What's the greatest milestone in your faith journey so far?

_____

_____

_____

_____

_____

TODAY'S PRAYER

_____

_____

_____

PRACTICE

What person, milestone, accomplishment, or answered prayer (large or small) needs to be celebrated?

_____

_____

_____

How will you celebrate it this week?

☐ Writing it down in your journal.

☐ Enjoying a cupcake.

☐ Setting a meaningful, tangible reminder in a place of importance.

☐ Other: _____

Margin

"Someday" isn't a day of the week.

I enrolled in technical writing during my junior year at Texas A&M University for two very superficial reasons: 1) It fulfilled one of many English credits without forcing me into discussions on literature I didn't really understand; and 2) It met in a building directly across the street from Chipotle. (I'm a sucker for burrito bowls.) So, imagine my surprise when I was introduced to something I now understand to be invaluable: the concept of whitespace.

Whitespace is simply the portion of the page left unmarked. It's the principle that keeps designers from covering every inch of a document with words and pictures. Whitespace leaves separation between the content. It makes what's most important stand out, and it creates visual balance. Are you seeing the life-lesson here?

In our minds, "adulting" somehow translates into filling up every minute of every day. I'm forever fighting the urge to type out one more email, to slip in one more appointment, decision, or project. There's always one more household chore needing attention or one more extracurricular activity for the kids to participate in. Sometime ago, my life ran out of space to the point I felt like I couldn't breathe. Even though I wholeheartedly loved Jesus, my family, and my job, I felt like I was drowning from the inside out, and it took some time to figure out why.

Simply put, my life didn't have any whitespace.

There was no breathing room. No margin for the unexpected or spontaneous. No elbow room to gracefully accommodate the challenges of motherhood, marriage, and a career. There was no room to enjoy friendships or to pursue my dreams. Even if my calendar wasn't full (which it usually was), my mind was.

Without breathing room, the treasures of our lives feel like inconveniences. By doing more, we are actually offering less.

For a long time, it was easy to blame shift. I called spinning a hundred plates at once responsibility. I shrugged my shoulders at our fast-paced culture and said, "It's just the way it is!" It took the Holy Spirit some time to show me the problem wasn't with my schedule, or even with what other people needed from me. The problem was with my heart. As a broken people in a broken world, we are prone to fill our lives with more commitments and more stuff. But, when our hearts are set right, they drive us to the one place that satisfies: Christ. And the funny thing is, when we are full of Him, there's plenty of room to breathe.

I used to laugh to myself when people advocated for margin and rest. It seemed completely impossible to me - for hundreds of reasons you already know, because you feel them too - but I'm here to tell you it's possible. The most impactful changes aren't huge and drastic; they are small and mostly consistent. So, this begs the question: where do we start? I don't have an exact formula or an exhaustive list, but here's where I started:

1. Master the phrase, "It can wait." Few things are as urgent as they seem. Text messages, email, laundry, deadlines, to-do lists, and even personal dreams feel pressing and urgent. Often, my own self-imposed expectations create the urgency, not true need. Everything can have a place and time, but it doesn't have to be all at once, and it doesn't have to be now. Giving ourselves permission to move something to the "it can wait" category is incredibly freeing.

2. Take a break from technology and social media. The biggest problem isn't the content (though the negativity can certainly add unnecessary stress). The reflex of checking it every minute we are still robs us of so much opportunity to live, breathe, and experience. Find a week, some weekends, or a few evenings to take a break.

3. Plan to not have plans. It's easy to use days off to tend to the business of life, or even to travel to fun places. While those things are good and helpful, they aren't necessarily restful. Add margin to your calendar by designating some evenings and weekends to specifically have no plans, and then honor your commitment.

Your soul will thank you.

SCRIPTURE

Proverbs 19:21; Isaiah 40:30-31

REFLECTION

1. How full is your life right now?

☐ Totally empty

☐ Still plenty of room

☐ Getting pretty full

☐ About to overflow

☐ Completely overflowing

2. What is keeping you from creating margin?

_____

_____

3. If you were given a day where you weren't allowed to do anything other than relax, how would you spend your day?

_____

_____

TODAY'S PRAYER

_____

_____

_____

PRACTICE

Right now, choose one of the above tips for creating margin and determine how you will try it within the next 7 days, then go ahead and shoot a quick text to a friend for some accountability.

Conflict

"Forgiveness is unlocking the door to
set someone free and realizing you
were the prisoner."
- Max Lucado

"Conflict" can bring up images of volatile situations or
hot tempers, and those certainly need immediate, direct attention, but most of the conflict I've experienced
in my leadership roles and personal relationships have
looked very different than overt arguing or yelling. I've
found conflict often disguises itself as hurt feelings,
shirked responsibility, clashes in personality or pref-
erence, or even gossip.

I must have been six years old or so when my first
memorable splinter indecent happened. By memorable, I'm not referring to how my finger acquired the
splinter, but rather the terrifying extraction process.
It was Grandmother vs. Splinter in her 1950's pink
bathroom. Most people in our family called her "Sissy," short for "sister" and a term of endearment, but it
always made me chuckle, because of all the things my
grandmother was, a sissy wasn't one of them. She was
strong, direct, and loving. And that's exactly how she
approached the splinter situation.

She sat me down as she pulled out a needle and little green bottle of Campho-Phenique — her favorite cure-all. (I will never forget the smell of Campho-Phenique — it would make your eyes water if you got too close!) For the life of me, I didn't understand why we couldn't just leave it alone. It wasn't that big, and it wasn't bothering me; yet Grandmother insisted it had to come out. I tried to be brave, but my lip quivered uncontrollably.

"Oh, Meredith, don't cry!" she said in a high-pitched, matter-of-fact tone as she closed in on my hand, "This won't hurt a bit and it will be over before you know it!" I was an obedient child, so I let her pry my finger from the death grip of my other hand. I closed my eyes, so I didn't have to actually watch her dig the splinter out, and I hate to admit it, but she was right. It really didn't hurt much. I mean, it wasn't exactly pain free, but bearable. Even for a six-year-old. And let's be honest, the shiny new Band-Aid was the best part.

Every good childhood includes a few epic splinter stories. It means we tried new things, fell down in the process, and lived to tell about it. Turns out, conflict and splinters have a lot in common. In the same way neglected splinters fester, become infected, and cause unnecessary pain, unresolved conflict breeds disunity and unnecessary emotional pain. While everyone knows it should be addressed, the thought of actually facing it head-on causes anxiety and straight up fear. As in, your tummy feels queasy and your palms get sweaty. (Well, maybe yours don't, but mine do!)

But hang on - there's some good news here: healthy conflict resolution is a learned skill, which means you can indeed learn it, and you can actually teach others as well. Every great leader has endured conflict and lived to tell about it. As the leader of your family, your organization, or your team, here are three "must-do's" when addressing conflict:

1. Deal with conflict exactly how you would a splinter: address it quickly, even if it hurts a little (or a lot). Waiting only produces bitterness in your heart and distance in the relationship.

2. Follow my grandmother's lead: be strong, direct, and loving. There's no room for high horses or personal agendas.

3. Plan how you will handle conflict in your family or with your team in advance. After all, whether you lay out the rules of engagement in advance or not, conflict is going to happen. You are better off prepared!

Jesus presents a pretty clear plan in Matthew 18[1] on how we should address conflict. It starts with going directly to the person who offended us, and then it's kind of like the old adage, "If at first you don't succeed, try, try again." No matter how much we know Jesus' way is best, there's often a big gap between what we know and what we do. My most natural self wants to do everything opposite of what scripture says. I want to talk through it (a.k.a. vent) to everyone but the person who hurt me. I want to move in the opposite direction when I see them coming, because I hate confrontation. I want to feel justified by my hurt and anger rather than being quick to forgive and extend grace.

I still regret some past poorly handled conflicts, mostly because I waited, avoided, or didn't respond in love, but I'm grateful for some wins too. The life of every leader includes a few epic conflict stories - it means we engaged in relationships with passion, were let down a few times, failed a few times ourselves, and lived to tell about it. It means we know what not to do. It means we've had some intimate reminders of our need to both give and receive grace.

Unity is a beautiful thing, and it's worth fighting for, especially in our families, on our teams, and in our close friendships. So, when a splinter appears, grab a needle and the Campho-Phenique, and get to work.

SCRIPTURE

Matthew 5:7; 23-24; Matthew 18:15-17;
Colossians 3:1-17

REFLECTION

1. What kind of conflict are you most at risk for experiencing at home, at work, and at church?

Failure to Communicate

2. Is there someone or a situation where you need to follow the above advice? What can you do this week to pursue forgiveness and reconciliation?

No

TODAY'S PRAYER

Let me *head of problems*

PRACTICE

How do you need to improve your approach for handling conflict in your leadership roles and in your personal relationships? Take a few minutes to jot down your thoughts, and then share them with a trusted friend.

Start early and often

Criticism

"Life is messy, hard and weird. We don't have to act surprised anymore."

- Mike Foster

I remember the first time a local ministry leader publicly criticized me. I'd never personally met him, he did not know me at all, and his opinion was based on false information, but nonetheless, he used his public platform to criticize me and actively turn people against me. I was in my late twenties and very early in the ministry role I held at the time. I remember feeling shocked that a fellow Christ-follower serving in the same community would behave so harshly. Once the shock wore off, I was devastated. Criticism can make us feel as though we aren't good at anything, which is why it's important to avoid the emotional ditch criticism digs. Part of me wanted to throw in the towel and quit. Between sobs, the Holy Spirit whispered, "Is this all it's going to take for you to give up?" Outwardly and publicly, I responded graciously and appropriately, but my internal response to this criticism exposed two hard-to-swallow realities: I cared way too much about what people thought of me, and my identity wasn't fully grounded in Christ, because if it was, I wouldn't have been shaken to the core. Those two things needed to be settled early on, in order for God to continue using me in Kingdom work because (as I now understand) criticism goes hand-in-hand with leadership. In fact, the only way to avoid criticism is to do nothing of value, but I don't want that for my life, and neither do you. We want to live lives of significance. We want to actually move the needle. So, criticism is going to come, and when it does, we need to know how to handle it.

Looking back, I'm actually grateful for the experience, because it lead me to confess my need for people's approval and to immerse my heart and mind in God's truth so my identity could find firm footing. Another pastor in the area came to visit me during that season, and he encouraged me to out-love and out-last my critics. I've never forgotten his advice.

Jesus was falsely accused and publicly criticized. At the end, you could probably say He had more critics than friends. He didn't swing at every pitch, though He certainly could have. Sometimes, He simply responded with silence. Why? Because He knew who He was, and He knew what he was there to do. It wasn't up for discussion in His mind, no matter what others thought or said, and addressing every criticism would have only been a distraction from what was most important.

We are humans with feelings, so negative feedback stings; it can even bring us to tears. I've really worked on it over the years, and it's gotten better, but there's something in my stomach that sinks a little when I receive a negative reaction to something I've said or done. Sometimes I respond with gratitude, refection, and application. Other times, I don't give it a second thought or even a response. The difference? My filter.

Experience has taught me to do the following when criticism comes:

1. Consider the source. Are they wise and trustworthy? Do they really know me? Was the information coming from a place of judgement or love? Not all criticism is created equal, and when we assign all of it equal value, it's crushing.

2. Look for the truth. Assess if there is any truth in the criticism. If I'm not sure, I ask a trusted friend to help me evaluate. Ask the question, "What can I learn?" If a behavior change is needed, change it. If not, set the information aside and move on.

3. Take the high road. True criticism is usually delivered harshly, and responding in kind is never helpful. Secure, confident people are free to focus on others, and while criticism stings, it doesn't have to shake us.

SCRIPTURE

James 1:19-20; Proverbs 15:1;
1 Peter 2:23

REFLECTION

1. What criticism have you held on to a little too long, and why?

I'm shy, my Voice is too anoing, self criticism

2. Who do you trust in your life to tell you the truth, even if it's tough?

Ashlay Leal James NE

TODAY'S PRAYER

Help me only hear the voice
of truth

PRACTICE

Who do you know who may be feeling the
sting of criticism right now? Take a moment to
pray for them, then shoot them an encouraging text, affirming their strengths and their value to you.

_____

_____

_____

_____

_____

_____

_____

_____

Hospitality

Somehow over the last decade, I became a bit confused about what hospitality actually is, much less why it's vital to our lives as Christ-followers. Because my schedule is full of meetings and people and lunch appointments, it's like I was mentally checking off the hospitality box without actually doing it. The more public my leadership roles have become, the smaller my personal life has become, and the last thing I want to do after the end of a long day is open my heart and home to people I don't know well. (How's that for honesty?) Plus, without actually putting it into words, I assumed the practice of regular hospitality was for Pinterest queens, super chefs, true extroverts, or people with a lot of free time. Because I meet exactly none of that criteria, I really didn't give it much thought until I studied the gospels through the lens of Jesus' relationships. Jesus practically ate his way through Luke! Every time you turn around, Jesus is having another meal - often with people He wasn't "supposed" to. And when He wasn't eating, He was incredibly intentional about moving toward people to heal them, to know them, or to just pull them in close. Jesus' lifestyle of hospitality not only shines a light on how we should do relationships, but on God's character and how He engages with us.

It's easy to confuse entertainment with hospitality, and for years, they've been the same in my mind. Entertainment isn't necessarily a bad thing, but its motivation is based on impressing, while hospitality is centered on serving. Entertainment shows off, while hospitality welcomes in. Entertainment brings pressure to straighten, plan, and keep up appearances. Hospitality is free to be vulnerable, transparent, and real. Entertainment follows an agenda. Hospitality listens. Entertainment is usually limited to an event, while hospitality is a way of life.

1 Peter 4:8-9 spells it out for us: *Above all, love each other deeply, because love covers a multitude of sins. Offer hospitality to one another without grumbling.*[1] How different would our lives be if we practiced every part of this verse? The "without grumbling" part really grabbed my attention because I've played the hospitality card without a happy heart many times.

I'm far from mastering any of this, but I'm glad to share what I'm learning.

1. Hospitality invites strangers. Between work and my family, I don't participate in many purely social activities. But when I do, I tend to reserve those precious few moments for friends - people I know, love, and miss. Which is a good thing. It's a fun thing, a necessary thing, a life-giving thing, but it probably isn't hospitality. Biblical hospitality usually refers to strangers - all the people who are NOT on our go-to list. Biblical hospitality moves us toward neighbors we don't know, the barista who finally learned to spell our name, and the homeless man on the corner we wave to every morning. And, it calls us to invite them in.

2. Hospitality invites people into the ordinary parts of our day. We eat. We drink coffee. We go places and do things. Hospitality opens the door wide and says, "Come with!" I'm learning this isn't about doing a 180-degree turn; it's more like a 10-degree course correction. I don't need to add a whole bunch of new things to my list, I just need to do what I'm currently doing differently. Our greatest asset isn't our charm or personality (thank goodness); it's our table. Inviting people to sit at our table invites them into our lives, into the truth of the Gospel, and into authentic community. We find common ground at the table. There's healing, encouragement, and restoration.

3. Hospitality calls us to invite others because we have been invited by God. It's far too easy to forget we are the stranger, the naked, the poor, and the powerless. But without Christ's redemption, that's exactly who we are. Somewhere in all of this we've established hierarchies and become comfortable with pointing fingers. Our forgetfulness is as old as sin itself, and over and over God pleads with us to remember how He invites us in, how He provides and strengthens, and how He is our only hope for rescue. True hospitality - God's hospitality - doesn't come from a place of obligation or quiet grumbling; it overflows from deep gratitude and humility, knowing we invite others in because we have been invited in by God Himself.

Seeing God's hospitality toward me, toward His people, stirs up things in my heart I'm not prepared for because they feel unnatural to me. There's a temptation to just keep things how they've been - it's easier and more comfortable. But when I stop and sit in the quiet, and when I'm honest with myself and with God, I want to be like Jesus - in His love, in His sacrifice, and in His hospitality.

SCRIPTURE

1 Peter 4:8-9; Romans 12:13;
Hebrews 13:1-2; Leviticus 19:33-34

REFLECTION

1. What false assumptions have you had concerning Biblical hospitality?

_____

_____

_____

_____

_____

2. How has God welcomed you in? How has His hospitality toward you changed you?

_____

_____

_____

_____

_____

_____

TODAY'S PRAYER

_____

_____

_____

PRACTICE

Brainstorm some simple ways to practice hospitality. Think through your recent acquaintances, and find a simple way to invite them in. List their name and your ideas below as a sign of your commitment to follow through.

_____

_____

_____

_____

_____

_____

_____

_____

Stewardship

"Tell me, what is it you plan to do with
your one wild and precious life?"
- *Mary Oliver*

A few days ago, a sticky note from around eight years ago slipped onto the floor as I shuffled some old files around. Right there, in my own handwriting, was a paraphrase of Psalm 24:1-2: *God made the world and everything in it. We are stewards not owners.* I've probably used thousands of sticky notes since then, and I couldn't tell you what was written on even ten of them most days, but I remember writing every single word on that pale-yellow piece of paper. I was on the very front end of one of the most thrilling and strenuous leadership adventures of my life and was totally overwhelmed by it all. Mounting pressure to build something from the ground up and to make a real impact made it hard to breathe. Sleep was hard to come by and the stakes felt incredibly high - both because I'd quit a job I loved to start a nonprofit during a terrible economic recession, and because there were so many desperate needs in our community. I knew this was God's assignment, but I'd let the burden of making it happen myself creep in. But then I read the beginning of Psalm 24, and I found freedom.

The earth is the Lord's, and everything in it, the world and all who live in it; for he founded it upon the seas and established it upon the waters.[1]

The work, the opportunities, the people, the needs, the resources, the organization, the platform, the reputation - none of it belonged to me. It was all His. It always had been, and it always would be.

Misplaced ownership is a slippery slope. When we think things in this world belong solely (or even mostly) to us, we run the risk of building our own kingdom instead of God's. Pride can trick us into thinking success by the world's standards means we've got it right, distracting us from what's eternal. When we get confused about who is really in charge here, fear easily creeps in, telling us to play too small and hold back because we don't see how more could even be possible, tempting us to quit when things get hard, or causing us to hold on so tightly to what's right in front of us we miss out what's to come.

Jesus tells an amazing story in Matthew 25[2] to reorient our perspective. A master was going on a journey, so he gathered his most dependable servants and entrusted his wealth to them for the duration of his absence. Before leaving, he gave one servant five bags of gold, another two bags, and finally another one bag. The first two servants invested what they'd been given and doubled their value, but the servant with one bag of gold buried it in the ground. The master eventually returned and proceeded to have two very different conversations. He affirmed and rejoiced with the two who had done something with what they'd been entrusted, saying "Come and share your master's happiness!" But the conversation with the servant who buried his one bag of gold had a completely different tone. The master didn't call him cautious or conservative. He called him lazy. Then, he took his bag of gold and gave it to the first servant.

The master clearly represents God, and we are the servants. So much of our role in this life is about stewardship. Reducing it to a mere collection of experiences, failures, or successes would be such a shame. We've been entrusted with a gift. We are stewards of this one life - this tiny blip on the continuum of eternity. God has handed us precious time, resources, talents, relationships, and opportunities, and He absolutely lights up when we do something with all He has entrusted to us.

Living and leading from the perspective of stewardship causes us to understand:

1. We are free from unnecessary burdens. There's comfort and freedom in not being the ultimate authority. We do not have to have all the answers because God has them.

2. We've been entrusted with great responsibility. It's a privilege to be invited into God's story, and good stewardship requires intentional investment on our part.

3. We've been entrusted with tremendous opportunity. We simply cannot imagine what God can do in us, through us, and around us. So, whether we risk our time, our careers, our dollars, or our reputation, seizing the opportunities He has placed before us is an important part of stewarding our lives well.

I don't want to waste my life on things that don't matter, and neither do you. When I reach the end of my time here on earth, I want to have poured out everything I've been given. Let's start with stewarding today well. And then, let's keep doing the same tomorrow.

SCRIPTURE

Matthew 25:14-29; Psalm 24:1-2;
Ephesians 2:10

REFLECTION

1. What burdens are you released from because God is the ultimate owner of the world and everything in it?

I don't have to make my own

ending

2. How does God entrusting you great responsibility and tremendous opportunity make you feel?

humbeled

TODAY'S PRAYER

_____

_____

_____

PRACTICE

Write one of today's scriptures in your own words.

everything is God's

and the has total control

_____

_____

_____

_____

_____

_____

_____

_____

Final Thoughts

Sharing these thoughts and stories with you has been a tremendous privilege. Honestly, there were a few stops along the way where I considered throwing the whole thing out because these words come from places of deep, raw vulnerability. But, since one of the chapters is about bravery and the whole idea of quitting fear, I thought I'd better press on.

There could have easily been twenty more chapters, because leading well is just that complex sometimes. And I'm sure you have your own stories - the ones being written with your life every day when you choose to show up and say, "Let's do this, God!"

I hope you feel the opportunity to lean in, because God is doing stuff and He is inviting you along. He is with you in the moments that are seen just as much as the ones unseen, and He dropped you on the planet at this time in history for His great purpose. Don't get caught up in the things that are temporary and distracting. Don't feel pressure to imitate the success of those around you. Keep your eyes locked on His and move forward one step at a time.

I confessed early on that I'm not an expert at any of this. None of us are. But there's a generation coming along behind who need two things from us: 1) They need us to lead from a firm foundation of truth and grace; and 2) They need us to cheer them on. So, as you take your own steps forward, grab a few hands and take them with you.

To close this stretch of our journey together, I thought it would be fitting to end where we started:

My dear friends —
Be steadfast.
Immovable.
Always abounding in the work of the Lord.
Knowing that in the Lord your labor is not in vain.

Acknowledgements

So many people influenced these pages by investing in my life. To each of you who helped shape these stories and who walked with me through learning these truths, I want to thank you. Your lives shine brightly, and I love Jesus more because of you.

Thank you, David, Abigail, Ella, Mom, and Dad for being patient with me while I sequestered myself in the upstairs office to work on this project. David, you've been cheering me on most of my life. Thank you for believing in my dreams. You are my very favorite. Mom and Dad, thank you for living lives of faith I want to follow.

Becca Collins, you've walked me through pages of scripture for years and your fingerprints are throughout this book. The same is true of my dear friend Susan Flippen. So much of what I know about leadership was learned from watching you (and I'm still learning!). Thank you for being with me and for me.

Leah Sequeira and Karen Gorski, thank you for being such faithful friends who pray confident, bold prayers. My life is so much richer because of you. Heather Celaya and Kara French, the road from childhood to adulthood has been sweeter because we've traveled it together. You two have always been up for my crazy adventures, and I'm so grateful. Michelle Harrison, your friendship came at the perfect time in my life. Your bold obedience and faith inspire me. I'm also grateful for your willingness to edit and give feedback! Leslie Carter, you are so dear to me. I couldn't be more thankful for your friendship and your leadership.

To the family of friends who are part of True To Life Ministries, I couldn't ask for a better tribe. David and I had no idea what God would do when we gathered a handful of folks around the dining room table years ago. You are transforming generations. Look at all God has done, and I'm confident there's so much more to come.

David King designed this beautiful book cover, and artwork from our daughter, Abigail, inspired the shape and style of the mountains – well done you two! Credit for the photo on the back cover goes to Kris Pounds Photography – thanks for sharing your talent!

Finally, I want to thank my new friends at Nyree-Press for providing outstanding support throughout this project.

> This book is dedicated to the
> True To Life Ministries Team.
>
> True To Life Ministries is a nonprofit organization committed to cultivating hope and introducing people to true life in Christ by providing the skills, resources, and community of support people need to change their lives as they transition out of poverty.
>
> Please take a few minutes to learn more about True To Life Ministries at
> www.ttlm.org.

About the Author

Meredith King is the Founder & Vision Ambassador of True To Life Ministries, a nonprofit organization committed to cultivating hope and introducing people to true life in Christ by providing the skills, resources, and community of support people need to change their lives. True To Life's work helps students and adults transition out of poverty and move toward self-sufficiency. True To Life has impacted thousands of lives and has become a resource for organizations across the country.

Meredith has dedicated her life to helping people get unstuck personally, professionally, and in their faith journeys. Meredith has mentored hundreds of leaders to grow their own leadership tools and to facilitate the creation of high-performing, self-managing teams. She is part of the senior leadership team at Integrus Leadership, an organization committed to providing leadership and organizational development solutions to Kingdom-minded leaders.

Meredith is a sought-after Bible teacher and is passionate about bringing God's truth to life through the humor and practicality of everyday experiences. She married her high school sweetheart, David, and life is now full and energetic thanks to two precious daughters and a lot of coffee. Meredith, David, Abigail, and Ella live in Texas.

You can connect with Meredith on social media and at www.meredithkingblog.com.

Endnotes

Chapter 1: Identity
1. Jeremiah 2:13, NIV.
2. John 7:37-38, NIV.

Chapter 2: Our Calling
1. See Romans 1:1-7; 1 Corinthians 1:7-9, 26-31; Ephesians 4:1-4; 2 Timothy 1:9. After researching this topic, I heard my friend Kat Armstrong preach an amazing message on the idea of calling vs. assignment, which helped solidify this concept for me. You can find Kat at www.katarmstrong.net.
2. See John 15:1-17.

Chapter 3: Your Calling
1. Ephesians 2:10, NIV.

Chapter 6: Prayer
1. See Matthew 18:2-4.
2. 1 Thessalonians 5:17, NIV.
3. Mark 1:35, ESV.
4. Luke 5:16, NIV.
5. Hebrews 5:7, ESV.

Chapter 7: Humility
1.Beth Moore, Living Free (Nashville: LifeWay Press, 2001), 44.

2. See Colossians 3:12.
3. See 1 Peter 5:5.
4. See Ephesians 4:1-2.
5. See Isaiah 66:2 and Proverbs 3:34.
6. Matt Perman, "What is the Role of an Elder?" Desiring God, January 23, 2006, www.desiringgod.org/articles/what-is-the-role-of-an-elder.

Chapter 8: Faith
1. See Hebrews 11:6.
2. See Mark 4:35-41.
3. Mark 4:40, NIV.

Chapter 9: Wisdom
1. James 1:5, HCSB.
2. James 3:15, HCSB.
3. James 3:14-15, HCSB.

Chapter 10: Bravery
1. See Luke 9:13.

Chapter 11: Multiplication
1. See Matthew 28:18-20.

Chapter 12: Failure
1. Note: The Practice activities were inspired by activities presented by Mike Foster in his book, Freeway. You can find more about Mike's work at www.peopleofthesecondchance.org.

Chapter 13: Words
1. See Matthew 5:14.
2. Philippians 2:14-15, NIV.

3. Tim Ferriss, "I Went 21 Days Without Complaining and It Changed My Life," Huffington Post, July 22, 2014, https://www.huffingtonpost.com/tim-ferriss/no-complaint-experiment_b_5610433.html.

Chapter 14: Friendship
1. Exodus 17:12, HCSB.
2. Beth Moore, Entrusted: A Study of 2 Timothy (Nashville: LifeWay Press, 2016), 40.

Chapter 15: Celebration
1. See Joshua 4.
2. Joshua 4:6, NIV.

Chapter 17: Conflict
1. See Matthew 18:15-19.

Chapter 19: Hospitality
1. 1 Peter 4:8-9, NIV.

Chapter 20: Stewardship
1. Psalm 24:1-2, NIV.
2. See Matthew 25:14-30.